Call Me Queequeg, Ishmael

ISBN 13: 979-8-9874213-1-4

Published by Agreement with Summerfield Publishing, New Plains Press, PO Box 1946, Auburn, AL 36831
publisher@newplainspress.com
newplainspress.com

R. Allen Shoaf 1948-

First Printing, 2023

Call Me Queequeg, Ishmael

R. Allen Shoaf

NewPlainsPress.com

Homage to Herman Melville

For Robert B. Shaw

CONTENTS

The following poems record my response to two of the many works by Herman Melville, *Moby Dick* and *Billy Budd*.

Recently, I resolved to read *Moby Dick,* in part because when 18 years old, I tried but could not finish it. I understand now why this was the case, but that is another story. This time I did finish the novel and then immediately read *Billy Budd*. Over the several months in which I was involved in this reading, and writing, I slowly became convinced that Melville, who left many thousands of pages of writing at the time of his death, was and is an authority, a true author, in the western tradition of what we can most conveniently describe as human self-examination.

Melville is adept at asking the sorts of questions that many people avoid like the plague. Why are we here? What are we going to do? Are we supposed to do anything? If so, who is the one doing the supposing? Is there really such a thing as civilization? If so, what can an individual contribute to it? If it does exist, why do so many allegedly civilized people destroy each other in so many different and often heinous ways? Why are we so full of hatred? Why can we hardly ever live together in peace? What drives us to do what we do? Why do we die?

These are hardly all the questions that Melville asks. But they are enough of such a list to lead us to what may be the more important realization. It is the way in which Melville asks the questions that move us, that leave us often shaken to the core. Some would call this his style. And certainly that's acceptable. But if we were tasked with describing this style, what would we say?

I think we would, and probably should, say that his writing is mag-nanimous, in many different senses, but especially in the sense of the opposite of stingy. Where some would accuse him of verbosity, uncon-trolled wordiness, another, of whom I am one, would say, instead, he pours out of his imagination, and his astonishing vocabulary, practically inexhaustible discourses for us of what it means to be human. It is to this style, if we want to call it that, that I've tried to respond with my poems—to be as magnanimous, as little stingy as I can be, as a way of celebrating one of the greatest writers I have ever encountered over my 75 years of life, more than 60 of them devoted to reading.

Please note that I am not a Melville scholar, an authority on the life and writings of Herman Melville. I am a reader of Melville. The one activity that has consumed my life and most of its energy is reading. And reading Melville has helped me craft in my poems what I have learned in that lifetime. I share my poems, my craft and my understanding in the pages that follow.

Subtle Knot

> *... in this world it is not so easy to settle these plain things. I have ever found your plain things the knottiest of all.*
> *~Moby Dick*

We're admonished to keep matters simple
When we know for sure they're anything but.
We do our best to untwist the cumbrance
Until all the lines, even where they cross,
Are plain to see, and we need no Ariadne
To make our way out of the labyrinth.

But in an instant one line snaps in two
And its mate recoils, whipping out of sight,
Leaving us at loose ends in flickering gloom
Where monsters confront us, mirrors in hand,
Far more menacing than the Minotaur,
Ready to deceive Daedalus himself.

Ask first of all who profits if it's plain.
Who gains the most from concealing the knot?
They're the ones fussing you should keep it simple.
They're the ones with agendas of deceit.
Keep your cool and quietly ignore them—
Your plain things are the knottiest of all.

So you work your way untying the knot,
Patiently separating the lines of thought,
Willing to grant it may not be deceit
But only the snarled indifference of nature
Unconcerned with your fingertips so raw.
Still, you must test the knot for yourself.

It's not so easy to settle these plain things
When the mysteries surface to awe you
With knots no Alexander will ever cut,
No sword so sharp of steel or intellect—
Only your courage to play out the lines
Until you can subtle the plainest knot.

Foreign to Nature

... Billy ... was yet by no means of a satirical turn. The will to it and the sinister dexterity were alike wanting. To deal in double meaning and insinuations of any sort was quite foreign to his nature.

~*BILLY BUDD*

Double meaning and insinuations,
The lingua franca of those we hardly trust,
Consume our spirits as they harden our minds
To care more for winning than for living.
Who enters the dance floor otherwise deceived?
After all, his intent, as we say, is to score.

Such cynicism, I hear you object,
As if I look for the worst in everyone.
Not so, I reply. I listen for good
And I celebrate it when I find it,
But living requires effort and not just luck
Where so many, too many, angle for luck.

They fall back on the sinister dexterity
Of the will to equivocate, words as weapons
Of sharpest edges, when a victim bleeds
Before he knows he's been cut, as in the words
Sinister, left, and *dexterity*, right,
Leaving us wounded in twice double meanings.

Oh, how difficult it is to listen!
To hear history's admonitions
Or Nature's whispers as well as her screams,
Cautions and lessons arrogance ignores
To its everlasting peril and pain
In this brief candle of a human life.

If once we should really hear the angel,
Our parable, and pay heed to the song,
We would fall to our knees and weep our thanks
For the gift to speak and say what we mean,
Expecting the like from the other in turn,
No malice in his cheek nor any in ours.

Against Cannibalism

I met a woman once—so beautiful
I still catch my breath in spasms of longing—
Who wrote a book on cannibalism:
You know (she told me) we don't have to be
Cannibals feeding on one another.

To this day (I'm steeped in years more than a few),
I hear and see her in this moment of grace,
And I almost cry I can't tell her how much
Her words and her beauty have buoyed me
In tempests that would otherwise have drowned me.

She befriended me in an hour so dark
I feared I'd never see the light again
(I still have the letter she wrote to me),
And through all these years I know in my flesh
I'm less a cannibal than I would've been—

Who can reckon the waves of desire
That crash against a man who cannot have
What he wants so much it mutilates him
Leaving him certain in an ocean of chance
Once there was a blessing he had to let go?

Harmless Harmony

> *... For what can more partake of the mysterious than an antipathy spontaneous and profound, such as is evoked in certain exceptional mortals by the mere aspect of some other mortal, however harmless he may be, if not called forth by that very harmlessness itself?*
> *~Billy Budd*

We excoriate the good and the beautiful.
We can't endure their reproach of our best
When simply being there they make it less.

We want them to suffer, to feel our pain,
Unable to rejoice in the light they shine
Envying their luck as if it were unearned

When this is to miss the whole point of luck
Since no one grabs Fortune's forelock really—
She's vanished before you even raise your hand.

We're most anxious, though, in our ambivalence
We may be using the wrong word for our fear
Of a mortal apparently harmless.

We once imagined a different category,
In times gone by, in various cultures.
Some figured it's not "luck" but "the grace of God"—

As if a god would meddle in a man
To mark him as somehow unusual,
Not by any choice but by simple being,

In which life, rising from the ocean's depths,
Evolves through affinities in earth emerging
Not by chance but elemental harmony.

Vengeance's Usury

"   Vengeance is mine, and retribution.   "
    Deut. 32:35

*And the retaliation is apt to be in monstrous dispropor-
tion to the supposed offence; for when in anybody was
revenge in its exactions aught else but an inordinate usurer?*
    ~Billy Budd

*... though man loved his fellow, yet man is a money-
making animal, which propensity too often interferes with his
benevolence.*
    ~Moby Dick

Once you give up integrity, the rest comes easy.
    ~J.R. Ewing

Look at it as book-keeping and remember
Nearly everyone cooks the books sometimes.
An eye for an eye hardly yields profits.
That's nothing but exchange, no money in that,
So up steps the usurer to fix it all,
And fix it he will, rest assured of that.

The quality of mercy may not be strained
But mercy's still a player in the game
And apportioned one way or another.
Someone has to pay. That's the law: not man's law,
Not god's, not nature's, but the universe's—
Strike that law and the quantum will rupture.

So you take my eye and I take your life.
Some serious usury, wouldn't you say?
Courts condemn such excess and sentence me,
Even in equity, to servitude
Corporal, fiscal, very likely both—
And the quantum fabric holds not rent.

Or that's the assumption by which we live.
Oh poor Billy Budd! Whoever! Wherever!
The rope around your neck links you and us
So tenuously to truth and justice
We clutch at strands to secure our interest
In the redemption "God bless Captain Vere."

Fanaticism

Nor is the history of fanatics half so striking in respect to the measureless self-deception of the fanatic himself, as his measureless power of deceiving and bedevilling so many others.
~Moby Dick

America died six years back, her corpse
Reanimated by hatred and greed.
A zombie now, she obeys greed's curses
As the wealthy eat the poor day and night
And excrete their waste in dying rivers,
No water fit to drink nor food to eat
Nor air to breathe unless you pay for it.

Endless pundits endlessly argue why
Since it gives them something to do with their time
And puts some jingle in their pockets, too—
What's not to like? The media frenzy
Only craves more of the same all the time
And is pleased to sacrifice the country
For headlines more lethal than pestilences.

So the people consume their own vitals
Deceived and bedeviled by infantile
Representatives who empty the word
Of all meaning since they represent no one
But themselves, ignoring their heritage,
Which would teach them the price of fanaticism:
Nothing to show for it but gross white blubber.

Your Law of Precedents

*And for years afterwards, perhaps, ships shun the place;
leaping over it as silly sheep leap over a vacuum, because
their leader originally leaped there when a stick was held.
There's your law of precedents; there's your utility of tradi-
tions; there's the story of your obstinate survival of old beliefs
never bottomed on the earth, and now not even hovering in
the air! There's orthodoxy!
~Moby Dick*

He's right, you know. We may not like it, true,
But he's right. Many are the times we sail
Into turbulence because tradition steers us,
When staying our course we'd reach safe harbor
And give thanks to sleep in our own beds
Far from the sea of sorrows, for one night at least,
Under coverlets not soaked in brine and blood.

Whether the brine and blood are real or fictive
We know what the figure is—Billy Budd
Hanged for conformity's sake. Our psyches,
Innocent also, swing from the yardarms
Of conformity from our earliest years
And we suffer throughout our lives to loosen
Knots which in the end strangle us all the same.

Oedipus stumbles toward Colonus blind,
Alone, cursed, fraught with meanings none but he
Can endure and continue to live on earth.
His death will hallow the ground and protect
Those who honor him for piety's sake.
The price of this honor and hallowing
Is his suffering our separation.

We none of us can return, untimely ripped
From her soft bosom. Piety demands
His sacrifice. Individuals each
We now wander in search of Leviathan,
So white, to boast our transcendence of her,
Even as she ceaselessly provides for us
So we can dismiss her with our pieties.

Little wonder Billy must hang, and soon—
Such beauty subverts our disdain of her.

"Platonian Leviathan"

What must we have read to understand this?
All world literature in all languages?

Some might mumble "Well, Hobbes, of course."
No, Hobbes is only a sociologist,

His Leviathan at most a metaphor
When we are talking about a sperm whale here,

Melville's "Platonian Leviathan,"
Capable of Spinoza if he liked.

Who cares? will be the most immediate scoff.
I propose Americans ought to care,

Not just because Melville is American
But because he had communed with the sea.

Around the world he had sailed the oceans
The mysteries of life boil hidden in,

And he was blood brother to loneliness
In the midst of men he knew how to love

(Queequeg, ... but also *Indomitable's* Chaplain
"Kissed the fair cheek of his fellow-man," Billy Budd).

I could almost call him our Odysseus,
The whale his destiny by Poseidon,

The fate that forced him to wander and search
Through thousands of words to find a return

Which never comes to pass in mortality,
Even should a man live many thousand years

And reach the Ithaka of his longing
Where Penelope waits to grace his bed

And show him the cave there's no escape from
As long as life divides for unity.

"How many ... have ... fallen into Plato's
Honey head, and sweetly perished there?"

You see, do you not? This Leviathan
Marks the end of man on land or sea.

It's no political order or system,
No totalitarian dream of power.

It's the sweetest "secret inner chamber
And sanctum sanctorum of the whale,"

Plato's honey head where ideas enchant
Unsuspecting seekers with visions sweet,

So sweet, none survives who hasn't sounded
The depth of division unity begets.

Futility

*"   ... the general stolidity discernible in the whole visible
world, which ... ignores you, though you dig foundations for
cathedrals.
~Moby Dick*

I've dug a few foundations in my life,
Even raised some walls, but none is now standing.
I ran out of time as all my friends died.

At my age to start another would raise
More eyebrows than any walls on the schedule,
And I'd likely end up digging my grave.

Still, I see my cathedral all around me,
Even if no one else does, and I imagine
Being buried within its close and keep.

Which I've learned is the most human response
To the world's general stolidity
And indifference to humanity

Since all other responses prove futile—
They weigh a man down with others' ideas,
The last thing he needs to dress his windows

For the stained-glass story of his life on earth,
The colors, shapes, and lead cames he means
For the cathedral he builds to save his crypt.

"manhood's pondering
repose of If"

If I had a nickel ... you know what I mean? ...
Every time I thought it'd be all right
And it turned out wrong, at best upside-down.

If I'd treated her better, just a bit ...
She would've been happy and stayed with me—
You can't give that much up for misery.

If I'd known how hard it is to get it right ...
I'd never have finished anything
Which would have been just as well. No one cares.

If I had not cared my clothes were ragged ...
I would have retreated even further
Into my imagination to survive.

If I had told the truth when I was hurt ...
They would have killed me and blamed me for it—
"Suicide, wouldn't you know it? Crazy," they smirk.

If I'd never have lit a cigarette …
My arrythmias wouldn't be so severe
Even though I quit forty years ago.

If I'd understood how sensitive she was …
I'd not have joined those brute 5th-graders
To pick on her and laugh when she wept.

If I'd have worked a little more with him …
My Corgi, bred though he was to herd cows,
Would've walked beside me against his nature.

If I'd listened to the mockery …
But I listened instead to poetry
And restless I repose pondering If.

Call me Queequeg, Ishmael

1

How do we cast out the outcast inside us?
Must we hunt the whale to find the monster?
Or is the monster the heart within us
We can't look on unless we look away,
Pretending we don't see ourselves in the mirror
That maims us every time we turn around
Hoping it's not there though we know better,
Its weight increasing no matter our curses
Or how passionate our prayers to the emptiness?
We ship, then, with Queequeg, each an Ishmael,
Hoping God has heard, doubting our return,
Hagar banished from Abraham's bosom
Through Sarah's jealousy all too human,
Though Hagar named God, he who has seen me,
She having seen Him, the first who named Him.

2

The seeing of God, to put it that way,
Asks for more than eyes. The terror of thirst,
Anguish for a child, the frenzy of despair,
The running back and forth in search of a well—
These sharpen the senses to madness's pitch
Which sees God seeing death seeing his carnage,

And this vision of God purges the fear
Gnawing Hagar's faith that she has seen God,
So she the outcast is the first to name God,
And she names Him "He who has seen me"
As she named her son "God has hearkened" to me.
And Ishmael boards the *Pequod* to see the sea
Which God has provisioned with Leviathan
So that all men of a mind to can see
God sees Ahab unworthy of his wife and son.

3

Not so Queequeg and Ishmael, friends beloved
One of the other, though they can't reproduce
And they must fall apart when Queequeg dies.
But such is his death his coffin remains
And serves as the womb that bears Ishmael alive
Through the devastation wrought by anger
And thirst for revenge which can never be slaked—
We almost hear "Call me Queequeg, Ishmael!"
As if God had hearkened to the men as one
And had seen in their brotherhood the love
Which makes men visible to God and God to men
If men will open their eyes to the man God makes
And into their hearts invite the outcast
Who used to live as if he owned the rights to life
But now lives a life owned by rites of love.

R. Allen Shoaf, or "Al" as most know him, published his fourth volume of poetry, *Language to Live In* in 2019. Previously, he had published *Simple Rules*, *Pied-Piper Philology: Love Words*, and *Erotic Reckonings*. In the past year, he published *Selected Poems 1968-2021*.

www.ingramcontent.com/pod-product-compliance
Lightning Source LLC
Chambersburg PA
CBHW020519160726
47991CB00007B/3029